THE GENTLEMAN'S GUIDE TO COCKTAILS

THE GENTLEMAN'S GUIDE TO COCKTAILS

ALFRED TONG

ILLUSTRATED BY JACK HUGHES

hardie grant books

This book is dedicated to Mohammed and Angela
for their support and friendship.

The Gentleman's Guide to Cocktails by Alfred Tong

First published in 2012 by Hardie Grant Books

Hardie Grant Books (UK)
Dudley House, North Suite
34–35 Southampton Street
London WC2E 7HF
www.hardiegrant.co.uk

Hardie Grant Books (Australia)
Ground Floor, Building 1
658 Church Street
Melbourne, VIC 3121
www.hardiegrant.com.au

British Library Cataloguing-in-Publication Data. A catalogue record
for this book is available from the British Library.

ISBN 978-1-74270-410-4

Art Direction & Design – Charlotte Heal
Illustrations – Jack Hughes
Design – Sergio Garcia
Colour reproduction by MDP
Printed in China by 1010 Printing International Limited

10 9 8 7 6 5 4 3 2 1

CONTENTS

INTRODUCTION

I once threw up in a Berkeley Square dustbin after drinking too many Flaming Ferraris. I drank them for a dare with my fashion-college chums at some Eurotrash nightclub in Mayfair. As I flicked a bit of stray vomit off the lapel of my jacket, I thought to myself, 'Never again'.

Cocktail culture, for many men, used to be something to ridicule. Ordering one was the kind of thing that an ageing lothario might do to impress a young girl. And perhaps because of the influence of *Sex and the City*, cocktails were also something for women and their gay friends. Now we have our own *Sex and the City* in the form of *Mad Men*.

Like other great American art forms such as jazz, cocktail culture reached its zenith in the 1950s. And like jazz, in 50s America, cocktails were enjoyed on a widespread scale, in their most rarefied form, by almost anyone who aspired to class and elegance.

It was a generation's rejection of these rituals that led us to Flaming Ferraris. Grandma and grandad, on the other hand, knew what they were doing when it came to a mixed drink. Now that we've grown up a bit (hopefully), we may find ourselves with swell gals in swanky bars. Or maybe important clients. So it's worth knowing how to conduct ourselves.

But isn't it all a bit of an effort, just to get a drink? Well yes, but then so is having a suit made, so is seducing a woman and so is landing a contract.

You wouldn't want to be a poor, badly dressed loner, so why be gauche when it comes to cocktails?

As with wine, or anything for that matter that requires a bit of knowledge, it is all too easy to be an insufferable bore when it comes to cocktails. It's a vast subject, full of tedious minutiae and not a little pretension. So I have decided to spare you.

There's a sense of theatre in a great cocktail bar that cannot be found in a pub. A cocktail can be dolce vita in a glass – the perfect accompaniment to an evening with a beautiful woman – or a lonely one-way ticket to vomit-flecked oblivion. Doing it properly matters.

THIS BOOK IS GOING TO SHOW YOU HOW.

PART ONE

CHAPTER 1
TOOLS OF THE TRADE

As with anything that requires a bit of kit – golf, espionage, sado-masochism, etc – it is easy to get carried away, but all you really need are a few essentials, many of which you will already have in your kitchen cupboard. The point is to get mixing, drinking and drunk, not accumulate useless bits of equipment.

Fridge Freezer

Ideally, get one of those American-style ones that dispense ice and have a bottle rack to increase the number of bottles your fridge can hold. Don't waste precious space in your drinks fridge on pointless things like food. A fridge freezer just for drinks and ice is the only way to go: one for your home and one for work, if possible.

Boston Shaker

Look for one with a metal top and a glass bottom. Glass conducts heat less effectively than metal and, therefore, will not dilute your drink as much, as the ice won't melt as quickly.

Bar Spoon

There's nothing wrong with just using a long spoon, chopstick or knife but a bar spoon looks the business, which always adds to the fun.

Spirit Measure

This is also happily known as a jigger. Vital for making evenly mixed drinks and also ones that include several different kinds of booze and, therefore, require more accuracy.

Pourer

An attachment that you add to your bottles to control the flow of liquid.

Juicer

Preferably a manual one as electric ones often break. Plastic ones have sharper ridges than glass ones.

Sharp Knife

For cutting, peeling and zesting fruit.

Blunt Instrument & Tea Towel

For bashing ice, or for crushing fruit and herbs together.

Hawthorne Strainer

Distinguished by a curved spring, this should fit flush onto the bottom part of your Boston Shaker.

Ice Bucket

An insulated ice bucket will keep your ice nice and ice-y for much longer.

Blender

For puréeing fruit, for instance peaches for a Bellini.

Measuring Glass

A big plain glass for mixing and measuring drinks.

GLASSES

Lord Byron used to drink out of a skull, patched up with bits of leather. German soldiers drank beer from a leather boot before heading out into battle. Here are some other drinking vessels you might want to consider.

TUMBLER

For short iced drinks like Old Fashioned and Negroni. Often referred to as an old fashioned after the drink.

HIGH BALL

For long iced drinks like G&T and Mojito.

CHAMPAGNE FLUTE

For champagne and champagne cocktails.

CHAMPAGNE COUPE

Not great for retaining fizz, but charming and often used for Margaritas.

MARTINI GLASS

For chilled drinks that are served without ice.

COLLINS GLASS

Originally used for gin-based drinks, but also good for tropical cocktails.

HURRICANE GLASS

Shaped like a hurricane lamp and best for exotic drinks.

CHAPTER 2
STORE CUPBOARD

Accumulating spirits for your basic home bar should be
a straightforward matter. It is possible to spend inordinate
amounts of money on fine vintage spirits, but they are
wasted in cocktails where they will be mixed with other
ingredients. Instead, invest in good-quality spirits and,
where appropriate, look beyond supermarket brands for
spirits with unique and complex flavours.

Gin

There are a number of specialty brands like No.3 London Dry Gin, which has juniper as its primary ingredient. It depends on your preference: some people like their gin to be quite fragrant, others dry. Plymouth, Tanqueray and Hendrick's are all perfectly good brands.

Vodka

Good vodka is good vodka, and Stolichnaya and Smirnoff, which are available practically everywhere, are perfectly fine. Expensive premium vodkas are generally not worth the extra money.

Rum

With rum it's worth looking beyond Bacardi – go for something with extra body and kick to it. Specialty brands like Diplomático have richer, more robust flavours while costing the same as Bacardi.

Whisky

There is no need to break out your 25-year-old malt whiskies for cocktails. Good bourbon is not only cheaper, its robust flavours are also generally more suited to making cocktails.

Tequila

Always have a good blanco or silver grade tequila tucked away.

Brandy

Brandy at its most rarefied is expensive and unnecessary for good cocktails. VSOP cognac and calvados will suffice.

Campari & Aperol

A lot of people ignore these but good bitters such as Campari and Aperol are essential to many cocktails. They are also great with sparkling wine.

Bitter

Always have a bottle of non-alcoholic bitters such as Angostura, Peychaud's and orange bitters handy.

Other Ingredients

Plenty of ice
Vermouth (Dolin or Noilly Prat)
Fresh oranges, limes, lemons, grapefruit
  and pineapples
Sparkling mineral water
Sparkling wine such as prosecco or cava
Tomato juice
Maraschino cherries
Sugar syrup
Grenadine
Mineral water
Soda water
Ginger beer

CHAPTER 3
PRINCIPLES, TIPS & TECHNIQUES

Contrary to what a mixologist or cocktailian might have you believe, fixing yourself a good cocktail needn't be difficult. Remember - it's just a drink. Simply bear in mind the general principles and instructions on the following pages.

BASIC PRINCIPLES

What makes a good cocktail?
Here is a short formula.

FOOD

1. A cocktail should whet the appetite or aid digestion.

+

STRENGTH

2. Strong, but not too strong. It should not knock you
out. Conversely, it should not have so much fizz and
fruit that it tastes like an alcopop.

+

THE SENSES

3. It should look, smell, sound and taste nice. Good,
fresh garnishes, chilled proper glasses, high-quality
ingredients and fresh ice.

+

COLD

4. Cocktails must be cooler than a polar bear's toenail
and colder than an Eskimo's graveyard.

=

SPLENDID DRINK

5. You should look at it, smell it, and finally drink it,
and think, 'Splendid!'

TIPS & TECHNIQUES

Relax

Avoid any bar-room acrobatics. It's just you making a nice drink for your friends.

Ice

You can never have enough good ice. In addition to ice trays, simply fill up a plastic container to make one huge ice cube that you can chip away at.

Glasses

Keep your cocktail glasses chilled.

Home-made syrup

It's just one part sugar and one part water, brought to the boil for five minutes. There's no need to buy it. Also, avoid things like sour mix for Margaritas.

Freshness

Always use fresh fruit and herbs.

Muddling

Muddling is simply using a blunt instrument to mash herbs so that they release their flavours.

Measuring

Use your jigger. A cocktail is a careful balance of flavours, so measurements do matter, especially with cocktails that use a number of ingredients.

Shaking and stirring

Just do as you're told. Shake when you're told to shake and stir when you're told to stir – it really does matter.

Take care of your ingredients

Vermouth, for instance, needs to be kept in the fridge and replaced after a month.

PART TWO

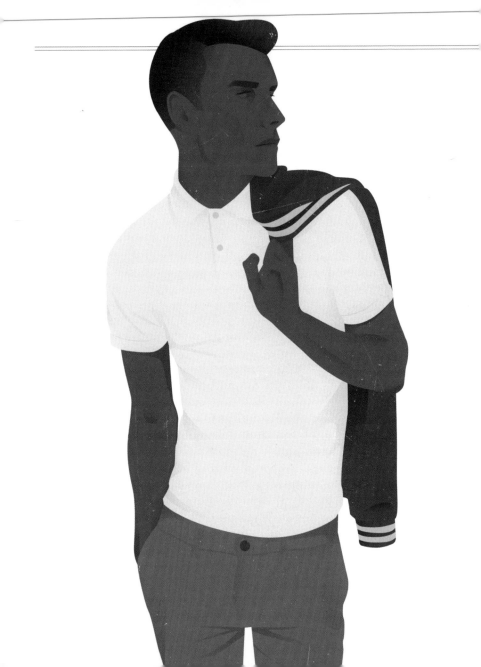

CHAPTER 4
COCKTAIL ETIQUETTE & DRINKING TIPS

In a world of bar chains and rowdy pubs a good cocktail bar is an oasis of relaxation and civility. But there are a number of things you should be aware of in order to get maximum enjoyment out of your cocktails.

FOOD

Ideally, cocktails should be drunk before or after a meal. So if you're inviting people out for evening cocktails suggest dinner before or after. And bear in mind, some drinks aid digestion and some whet the appetite.

Rufus' Reviver

Ingredients

50 ml (1 oz) rye whisky
50 ml (1 oz) Italian amaro (e.g. Nonino)
twist of lemon peel, to garnish

Method

Stir the whisky and amaro in a mixing glass with ice. Strain into a chilled martini glass. Top with the lemon peel.

DO YOUR RESEARCH

Whether you have been invited out for cocktails or are planning to invite others, do your research. What is the dress code? What is the house specialty? Who is the head barman? Where are the bathrooms? What is the general atmosphere? Ideally, you should have been to the bar first before inviting others: this means you can tell your guests what to expect and make them feel comfortable. If you have been invited out, try to go there first. At the very least look at the establishment's website.

Negroni

Ingredients

25 ml (1 oz) dry gin
25 ml (1 oz) sweet vermouth
50 ml (2 oz) Campari
twist of orange peel, to garnish

Method

Stir the ingredients with ice and strain into a tumbler filled with ice. Garnish with the orange peel.

KNOW THE BASICS

You should have some idea of the kinds of drinks that are served in a good cocktail bar and also how you like yours prepared. Do you prefer Dirty Martinis to dry ones? What kind of gin or whisky do you like? Bourbon, rye and Scotch have profoundly different qualities. Gins can range from the fragrant Tanqueray to the dry Gordon's. If you are not sure, ask how the house makes it or ask the barman what he suggests. Also ask him the reasons for this. Don't feign knowledge.

Gentleman's Agreement

Ingredients

40 ml (1½ oz) bourbon
15 ml (½ oz) brandy
15 ml (½ oz) crème de menthe
soda water
twist of lemon peel, to garnish

Method

Pour the bourbon, brandy and crème de menthe into a highball glass filled with ice. Top with soda water and garnish with the lemon peel.

BEFRIEND THE STAFF

Building up a rapport with the staff not only means you get better service but also helps you to become a more sophisticated and accomplished cocktail drinker. Ask questions about their job. Ask why they are doing things in a particular way or why they are using specific ingredients. If there is a bottle of spirits that you have not seen before, ask what it is.

Suleiman the Magnificent

Ingredients

25 ml (1 oz) rye whisky
25 ml (1 oz) cognac
25 ml (1 oz) sweet vermouth
½ teaspoon Bénédictine
dash of Peychaud's bitters
dash of Angostura bitters
maraschino cherry, to garnish

Method

Stir the ingredients together in a mixing glass filled with ice for 20 seconds. Strain into an ice-filled tumbler. Garnish with a maraschino cherry.

DRESS CODE

Cocktail bars should be low-lit so that faces are cast in the most flattering light. You should, also, focus on what is going on above the waist: a well-tailored jacket in a dark colour, a lightly coloured shirt, a simple textured tie and perhaps a pocket square to add flourish. This will be appropriate in most establishments. As Catherine Hayward, fashion director of *Esquire* advises, you should look 'thoughtful but definitely not try too hard.'

Boulevardier

Ingredients

50 ml (2 oz) bourbon
25 ml (1 oz) sweet vermouth
25 ml (1 oz) Campari
twist of orange peel, to garnish
maraschino cherry, to garnish

Method

Stir the ingredients with ice and then strain into an ice-filled tumbler. Garnish with the orange peel and maraschino cherry.

GETTING THE BARMAN OR TABLE SERVICE'S ATTENTION

Attract the attention of the barman or table service with eye contact, a smile or an arched eyebrow. On no account wave money, click your fingers or shout.

Manhattan

Ingredients

75 ml (2¾ oz) bourbon
25 ml (1 oz) sweet vermouth
2 dashes of Angostura bitters
maraschino cherry or twist of lemon
   peel, to garnish

Method

Stir the ingredients in a mixing glass over ice. Strain into a chilled martini glass. Garnish with a maraschino cherry or a twist of lemon peel.

RETURNING DRINKS

If you like a drink served in a particular way, ask politely but don't be pedantic. A drink can be replaced or changed, if it is tasted, disliked and rejected immediately.

Rupununi

Ingredients

50 ml (2 oz) El Dorado rum
teaspoon spiced honey
dash of Wray & Nephew rum
juice ½ lime, freshly squeezed
slice of lime, to garnish

Method

Shake and strain into a rocks glass with a slice of lime and crushed spices on top.

Recipe courtesy of Nightjar

ORDERING DRINKS FOR OTHERS

You may be called upon to order a drink for your companions. Base your decision on the spirit they tend to drink. So choose a Manhattan if you've noticed they like whisky. If they are novice drinkers suggest something light, refreshing and simple, like a Kir Royale or a Gin Fizz. Do not order strong cocktails for someone who isn't used to them. Never order a drink that you have never tried before for someone else.

Lady P's Pink Gin Fizz

Ingredients

50 ml (2 oz) Tanqueray gin
25 ml (1 oz) lemon juice, freshly squeezed
½ dessertspoon caster (superfine) sugar
soda water, to top
3 dashes of Angostura bitters
2 lemon wedges, to garnish

Method

Pour the gin and lemon juice into a mixing glass. Add the sugar, stirring it into the mix until it's completely dissolved. Fill a tumbler with ice, add the mix and top with soda until full. Add the bitters and garnish with the lemon wedges. Stir before serving.

MAKING A TOAST

When making a toast with cocktails, the clanking together of full glasses complete with garnishes can lead to spilled drinks. Far better to raise your glass in your companion's direction and make meaningful eye contact. It goes without saying that you should wait for all the drinks to arrive before you start drinking.

Gimlet

Ingredients

50 ml (2 oz) gin
10 ml (⅓ oz) lime juice, freshly squeezed

Method

Shake the ingredients vigorously with ice and strain into a martini glass.

SIP AND SAVOUR

A three-Martini lunch à la *Mad Men* may seem like a good idea. But if you're a cocktail novice it most certainly is not. It will get you very drunk, very quickly and in a manner that is entirely unpleasant. Cocktails such as Martinis are relatively short drinks that pack one hell of a punch. So go easy. One every forty-five minutes or so is about right.

Martini

Ingredients

50 ml (2 oz) gin
1 teaspoon dry vermouth
cocktail olive, to garnish

Method

Shake or stir (depending on preference
or 00 status) the gin and vermouth with
ice cubes, then strain into a martini glass.
Garnish with a cocktail olive.

Whisky Smash

Ingredients

50 ml (2 oz) bourbon
½ tablespoon caster (superfine) sugar
1 tablespoon water
2 sprigs of mint, to garnish

Method

Stir the ingredients in a mixing glass with
ice. Serve in a tumbler over ice. Garnish
with the sprigs of mint.

Cherry Champagne

Ingredients

50 ml (2 oz) cherry brandy
100 ml (4 oz) champagne

Method

Combine the ingredients in a champagne
flute and serve.

CHAPTER 5
LITERATURE, TELEVISION & FILM

The golden age of cocktail drinking was the 1940s and 1950s. Happily, this coincided with the golden age of Hollywood. Much of the mystique and glamour of the cocktail comes from this period.

In literature, the story is a little different. Authors prefer to write about wine and beer. Wine lends itself to all kinds of metaphorical flourishes – blood of Christ and all that – while beer is the drink of the working-class hero. All of which is gin and tonic to the worthy novelist. Cocktails tend to be the stuff of comedy and tawdry glamour.

In both contexts, cocktails have played a key role in signifying a character's personality traits and as a plot device. Copying your cinematic or literary hero by ordering their cocktail is usually best avoided. Nothing will make you look more stupid in a bar than to ask for your Martini shaken rather than stirred. But it is rather good fun.

So in that spirit, here are some iconic cocktails from literature, film and television.

GODFATHER II

In *The Godfather I*, Fredo gets told off by Mo Green for 'banging cocktail waitresses two at a time'. In *The Godfather II*, Fredo's Banana Daiquiri speaks of his inherent weakness as a man (let alone, heir to a huge criminal empire), which gives a vital clue to the upcoming betrayal of his cold-blooded brother, Michael, who drinks club soda – straight up.

Banana Daiquiri

Ingredients

1 ripe banana
50 ml (2 oz) rum
1 tablespoon Triple Sec
50 ml (2 oz) lime juice
1 teaspoon caster (superfine) sugar
maraschino cherry, to garnish

Method

Mash the banana in a mixing glass and add crushed ice. Mix with the rum, Triple Sec, lime juice and sugar. Shake vigorously. Strain and pour into a cocktail glass. Garnish with a maraschino cherry.

UNCLE FRED IN THE SPRINGTIME

The master chronicler of upper-class British buffoonery, P. G. Wodehouse, famously loved booze. And when it comes to cocktails, Bertie et al do not disappoint. 'To-morrow'll be of all the year the maddest, merriest day, for I'm to be Queen of the May, mother, I'm to be Queen of the May' is the full name of Lord Uffenham's cocktail in *Uncle Fred in the Spring Time*, which he believes will alleviate the deepest despondency.

The May Queen

Ingredients

1 glass of dry champagne
25 ml (1 oz) liqueur brandy
25 ml (1 oz) Armagnac
25 ml (1 oz) Kümmel
25 ml (1 oz) Yellow Chartreuse
some stout, to taste

Method

Stir the ingredients over ice and serve in a highball glass. Top up with stout.

It's not only the British upper classes who love a cocktail, the aspirational working classes do too – and none more so than Del Boy.

Caribbean Stallion

Ingredients

25 ml (1 oz) tequila
25 ml (1 oz) Malibu
25 ml (1 oz) crème de menthe
smidgen of Campari
merest suggestion of Angostura bitters
grapefruit juice, to taste
slice of orange, to garnish
wedge of lime, to garnish
seasonal fruits, to garnish

Method

Stir the ingredients over ice in a mixing glass, strain into a highball glass and garnish with a slice of orange, a wedge of lime, some seasonal fruits, a decorative plastic umbrella, two translucent straws, and voilà!

CASINO ROYALE

James Bond was a literary hero long before he was a cinematic one. In the book *Casino Royale*, he orders this variation on the Martini at the Dukes Hotel bar in London and names it after the character Vesper. Unsurprisingly, given their doomed romance, it's the only one he ever drinks. Attention cocktail bores: note how it's plain old Gordon's gin, nothing fancy.

Vesper Martini

Ingredients

75 ml (2¾ oz) Gordon's gin
25 ml (1 oz) vodka
15 ml (½ oz) Kina Lillet
twist of lemon peel, to garnish

Method

Shake the ingredients well and strain into a martini glass. Garnish with the lemon peel.

THE BIG LEBOWSKI

A man attempts to sip a creamy drink while being strong-armed by some thugs. 'Careful man,' he says, 'there's a beverage here ...' And so begins a cocktail cult that lasts to this day. The man in question is 'The Dude', and the beverage is a White Russian aka Caucasian. He drinks no less than nine during the film.

White Russian

Ingredients

50 ml (2 oz) vodka
50 ml (2 oz) single (light) cream
50 ml (2 oz) Kahlúa

Method

Shake the ingredients with ice and strain into a tumbler with ice cubes.

BREAKFAST
AT TIFFANY'S

When Holly Golightly was intent on leaving a party 'very drunk indeed', then the Zombie cocktails she was knocking back were sure to do the trick. Astonishingly designed as a hangover cure by restaurateur Donn Beach in 1934, with its four shots of rum this recipe would surely have had the opposite effect.

Zombie

Ingredients

25 ml (1 oz) light rum
25 ml (1 oz) golden rum
25 ml (1 oz) Jamaican rum
generous squeeze of lime juice
2 dashes of passion fruit juice
2 dashes of pineapple juice
sugar syrup, to taste
20 ml (¾ oz) overproof rum

Method

Pour the first three rums into a shaker and add the lime juice. Add two dashes of the fruit juices and one dash of sugar syrup (to taste). Shake vigorously and strain into a highball glass filled with ice. Float the overproof rum on top.

CASABLANCA

Because of *Casablanca* champagne cocktails must forever be drunk while conducting a doomed romance with a femme fatale. But not before reciting the most famous toast of all time, 'Here's looking at you, kid'.

Champagne Cocktail

Ingredients

1 sugar cube
2 dashes of Angostura bitters
25 ml (1 oz) brandy
90 ml (3 oz) dry champagne, chilled

Ingredients

Place the sugar in the bottom of a champagne flute with the Angostura bitters. Add the brandy and top up with champagne.

THE GREAT GATSBY

In a novel that is so evocative of New York, it might seem strange that Daisy fixes her cruel husband, Tom, a Mint Julep. Strange, that is, until you remember she is from Kentucky where the Mint Julep was invented. The subsequent Julep-fuelled binge ends in heartbreak and disaster for our man Gatsby. So beware flighty girls bearing Mint Juleps.

Mint Julep

Ingredients

5–6 mint leaves
1 tablespoon sugar syrup
75 ml (2¾ oz) bourbon
sprig of mint, to garnish

Method

In tumbler, muddle the mint leaves with the sugar syrup, and add crushed ice and bourbon. Garnish with a sprig of mint.

MAD MEN

Cocktails in *Mad Men* are not only used to evoke the era but also as comic and plot devices. Two cocktail moments spring to mind immediately: first, when Don Draper makes Conrad Hilton an Old Fashioned, which leads to the award of the Hilton Hotel advertising account, and second, when Roger Sterling throws up a bellyful of Martini and oysters in full view of a client.

Old Fashioned

Ingredients

1 brown sugar cube
3 dashes Angostura bitters
1 tablespoon soda water
50 ml (2 oz) bourbon
twist of orange peel
maraschino cherry, to garnish

Method

Dissolve the sugar cube in the Angostura bitters and a tablespoon of club soda and the bourbon in a tumbler. Add the orange peel and muddle everything together. Add ice cubes and garnish with a maraschino cherry.

CHAPTER 6
SEMIOTICS & STYLE

Like it or not, your cocktail will have something to say about you. But whether you should let this affect your choice of drink is an entirely different matter. Drink whatever you bloody well please. It is, however, worth being aware of some general rules and trends. After all, a gentleman never offends unintentionally.

The stylish men and women in the following chapter demonstrate that their choice of drink is not defined by their sex, sexuality or by fashion, but by what they think tastes good. And nothing can be more stylish than that.

THE SEMIOTICS
OF COCKTAILS

Speaking very broadly, light, sweet drinks like Mojitos and Cosmopolitans are the preserve of women. Dark, complex drinks like Negronis and Old Fashioneds are considered men's drinks.

Cosmopolitan

Ingredients

50 ml (2 oz) vodka
25 ml (1 oz) Triple Sec
25 ml (1 oz) cranberry juice
wedge of lime, to garnish

Method

Shake the ingredients with ice and strain into a chilled martini glass.

Long Island Iced Tea

Ingredients

25 ml (1 oz) vodka
25 ml (1 oz) gin
25 ml (1 oz) light rum
25 ml (1 oz) tequila
25 ml (1 oz) lemon juice, freshly squeezed
25 ml (1 oz) orange liqueur
1 teaspoon caster (superfine) sugar
75 ml (2¾ oz) Coca-Cola
slice of lemon, to garnish
slice of lime, to garnish

Method

Pour the ingredients into a highball glass full
of ice and stir. Garnish with a slice of lemon
and lime, and serve with a swizzle stick and
two tall straws.

Rob Roy

Ingredients

25 ml (1 oz) vodka
50 ml (2 oz) scotch whisky
40 ml (1½ oz) sweet vermouth
4 drops Angostura bitters
orange peel, to garnish
maraschino cherry, to garnish

Method

Stir the ingredients over ice and strain into
a chilled martini glass. Garnish with orange
peel and a maraschino cherry.

Order your drinks according to the venue and the occasion. If you are in a loud, fun Tiki bar have a Piña Colada, if you're in the Savoy, a Martini.

Bourbon Highball

Ingredients

50 ml (2 oz) Bourbon
ginger ale
twist of lemon peel, to garnish

Method

Pour the bourbon into an ice-filled highball glass, top up with ginger ale and garnish with the twist of lemon.

White Lady

Ingredients

50 ml (2 oz) gin
dash of lemon juice, freshly squeezed
dash of Triple Sec
1 egg white

Method

Mix the gin and lemon juice, and add the
Triple Sec and egg white. Shake over ice and
strain into a chilled martini glass.

Americano

Ingredients

25 ml (1 oz) Campari
25 ml (1 oz) Sweet Vermouth
soda water
slice of orange, to garnish

Method

Pour the spirits over ice into a highball glass,
stir and top up with soda water. Add the
orange slice.

Ultimately, you should let your taste buds, mood and the occasion decide. If the company you keep thinks less of you because of a perceived cocktail faux pas, then you should find new friends, not a new drink.

Planter's Punch

Ingredients

50 ml (2 oz) dark rum
25 ml (1 oz) lime juice, freshly squeezed
dash of sugar syrup
2 dashes of Angostura bitters
soda water
lime wedge, to garnish

Method

Shake the rum, lime juice, two dashes of Angostura bitters and sugar syrup over ice. Strain into a highball glass filled with ice. Top up with soda and garnish with a lime wedge.

Cuba Libre

Ingredients

50 ml (2 oz) white or golden rum
Coca-Cola
1 lime

Method

Pour the rum and Cola into a highball glass,
cut the lime into quarters, squeeze into the
glass and stir.

Dubonnet

Ingredients

50 ml (2 oz) Dubonnet
25 ml (1 oz) gin
twist of orange peel, to garnish

Method

Stir the ingredients over ice and strain into
a frosted martini glass. Garnish with a twist
of orange peel.

FAVOURITE MIXES
OF STYLISH PEOPLE

JEREMY LANGMEAD
Editor-in-Chief, Mr Porter

Dirty Martini

Ingredients

50 ml (2 oz) gin
2 teaspoons dry vermouth
1 teaspoon olive brine
1 lemon wedge
3 green olives (or to taste)

Method

Shake the gin, dry vermouth and olive brine over ice. Rub the rim of the cocktail glass with the wedge of lemon. Strain, pour into the cocktail glass and add the olives.

'I think Dirty Martinis are delicious and drinking one makes me feel like I have had drinks and dinner at the same time. That leaves more time for drinks. I drank my first one twenty years ago but rediscovered them again with much enthusiasm last year.'

GORDON RICHARDSON

Creative Director, Topman

Aviation

Ingredients

50 ml (2 oz) Beefeater London Dry Gin
25 ml (1 oz) lemon juice, freshly squeezed
15 ml (½ oz) maraschino liqueur
1 teaspoon crème de violette

Method

Shake the ingredients well, over ice and strain into a chilled cocktail glass.

'I like any cocktail with a gin base. One of the most memorable ones I've drunk was an Aviation cocktail. The very name evokes the days when it was exciting and very glamorous to fly. I first had one in New York in the Flatiron Lounge. Most cocktails can be a bit cloying and overpowering but the Aviation is a subtle, well-balanced mix of ingredients that, if made correctly, has the palest of pale blue hue – something that looks as stylish as it tastes.'

CATHERINE HAYWARD
Fashion Director, *Esquire* (UK)

Moscow Mule

Ingredients

juice of ½ a lime, freshly squeezed
50 ml (2 oz) vodka
100 ml (3½ oz) ginger beer

Method

Squeeze the lime into a tall glass (or Moscow
Mule mug), then toss in the used shell. Add 2
or 3 ice cubes and the vodka. Top up with cold
ginger beer and stir.

*'I would have to say one of my favourite cocktails
is the Moscow Mule. I ordered one on my first
date with my husband at LoungeLover in East
London. It's a mildly stimulating mix of my
favourite ingredients – lime, ginger beer and
vodka. Poured over crushed ice, it's so clean
and refreshing, you can almost kid yourself it's
non-alcoholic and, therefore, good for you.
I always feel energised after drinking one –
but not two. That's when you realise its hidden
strength. It feels like such an innocent cocktail,
but with hidden depths.'*

ALAN FLUSSER
Author, *Style and the Man*

Bull Shot

Ingredients

50 ml (2 oz) vodka
75 ml (2¾ oz) chilled beef bouillon
dash of Worcestershire sauce
dash of Tabasco
salt and pepper, to taste
celery salt (optional)

Method

Shake the ingredients well over ice and strain into a highball glass filled with ice.

'My favourite cocktail is a Bull Shot. It's a rare bird to come across, as the only bartenders familiar with this Old World drink are those over fifty, who have made a career out of tending bar for gentlemen. I don't think that there are more than six or so restaurants in all of New York that feature the drink. And, not ironically, they happen to be the most stylish classic venues still in business. It's kind of a drink out of the 1930s. As a matter of fact, if a restaurant serves the drink, you can bet they know high-class food and have a reputation for fine service.'

CHRISTOPHE LEMAIRE
Creative Director, Hermès

Whisky Sour

Ingredients

50 ml (2 oz) bourbon whisky
2 dashes of Angostura bitters
1 tablespoon cherry juice
50 ml (2 oz) lemon juice, freshly squeezed
50 ml (2 oz) sugar syrup (or to taste)

Method

Add the ingredients to an ice-filled shaker.
Shake hard and strain into a tumbler full of ice.

'I like Whisky Sours and had one for the first time last September on the terrace of a lovely, old-fashioned hotel in Catalonia. It was a bit empty and I was watching the sun set on the beautiful waters of the Mediterranean. The fresh softness of the drink, with a twist of danger was just perfect at that precise moment.'

OLIVIA INGE
Supermodel

Olivia's Fatty Bum Baileys Cracker

(serves 4)

Ingredients

2 bananas
half bottle of Baileys
4 scoops of full-fat vanilla ice cream
  (preferably Häagen Dazs)

Method

Whizz the ingredients up and pour into
four very large glasses. Drink while sitting
in the sun.

*'I have a sweet tooth and I love the ingredients
– bananas, Baileys, ice cream – it's a bit like
chocolate and it gets you merry when you think
you're just sipping on a milkshake. The overall
effect is that my milkshake brings all the boys
to the yard ... damn right, it's better than yours.'*

PART
THREE

CHAPTER 7
CLASSIC BARS

The origins of some of the most popular cocktails can be traced back to historic establishments still in operation today. These are the undisputed heavyweight champions of the bar world and remain some of the most wonderful places in the world in which to enjoy a cocktail.

AMERICAN BAR, THE SAVOY

London

Opened in 1898, the American Bar is responsible for introducing Europe to the delights of the cocktail. Its head barman, Harry Craddock, was the most celebrated of the 1920s and 1930s, inventing a number of cocktails including the White Lady.

White Lady

Ingredients

50 ml (2 oz) gin
25 ml (1 oz) Triple Sec
25 ml (1 oz) lemon juice, freshly squeezed

Method

Shake the ingredients vigorously over ice and strain into a chilled cocktail glass.

LONG BAR, RAFFLES HOTEL

Singapore

Set in the white stucco splendour of the Raffles Hotel in Singapore, the Long Bar is the home of the Singapore Sling. Invented by Ngiam Tong Boon in 1910, the Raffles version of this cocktail is still considered to be the best and has been enjoyed by the likes of Rudyard Kipling, Noël Coward, Joseph Conrad and Charlie Chaplin.

Singapore Sling

Ingredients

50 ml (2 oz) gin
25 ml (1 oz) cherry brandy
25 ml (1 oz) lemon juice, freshly squeezed
1 teaspoon grenadine
soda water
maraschino cherry, to garnish

Method

Shake the gin, cherry brandy, lemon juice and grenadine vigorously with ice. Strain in a tumbler over ice and top up with soda water. Add a maraschino cherry to garnish.

KING COLE BAR, ST. REGIS

New York

While the origins of the Bloody Mary are unclear, the King Cole Bar in Manhattan has a better claim to it than most. Although it went under the name of Red Snapper here, the barman Fernand Petiot created the version we are familiar with today by giving the Bloody Mary its characteristic spicy kick.

Bloody Mary

Ingredients

dash of Tabasco
dash of Worcestershire sauce
50 ml (2 oz) vodka
splash of dry sherry
150 ml (5 oz) tomato juice
25 ml (1 oz) lemon juice, freshly squeezed
pinch of celery salt
pinch of cayenne pepper
celery stick or slice of lemon, to garnish

Method

Pour the Tabasco and Worcestershire sauce over ice in a shaker and add the vodka, dry sherry, tomato juice and lemon juice. Season with celery salt and cayenne pepper. Shake vigorously and strain over ice into a highball glass. Garnish with a celery stick or a slice of lemon.

HEMINGWAY BAR, HOTEL RITZ

Paris

Again, it is unclear who invented the Sidecar. The Hemingway Bar boasts a story that is more convincing than most. Legend has it that the cocktail was created for a regular who always rode in on a motorcycle with a sidecar. The hotel mixes both the regular Sidecar and a deluxe version that uses Ritz Champagne Cognac 1865, which, as you can imagine, is one of the most expensive cocktails you may ever drink.

Sidecar

Ingredients

50 ml (2 oz) brandy
25 ml (1 oz) Triple Sec
twist of orange peel, to garnish

Method

Shake the brandy and Triple Sec over ice, strain into a tumbler filled with ice and add the orange peel to garnish.

AMATO'S RESTAURANT,

Formerly Julio Richelieu Saloon

Martinez, California

The barman Julio Richelieu of the Julio Richelieu Saloon fixed the first version of the Martini between 1862 and 1871. Legend has it a miner who had just struck gold wanted to celebrate with champagne but was instead given a Martinez Special – a slightly sweeter version of the drink we all know and love.

Martinez Special

Ingredients

50 ml (2 oz) sweet vermouth
25 ml (1 oz) gin
2 dashes of maraschino cherry juice
dash of bitters
twist of lemon peel, to garnish

Method

Shake the ingredients over ice, strain into a chilled martini glass and serve with a twist of lemon peel.

TRADER VICS,
Formerly known as Hinky Dinks
Oakland, California

There are two claims to the origins of the Mai Tai and neither of them are Polynesian as its name might suggest. The more popular story is that in 1944, Victor J. Bergeron fixed some friends visiting from Tahiti a special drink. One sip was enough for them to declare 'Maita'i roa!', which means, 'Out of this world!' in Tahitian. The other comes from his archrival Donn Beach who popularised Tiki-themed bars and restaurants, and claims to have made the first Mai Tai in 1933.

Mai Tai

Ingredients

50 ml (2 oz) Demerara rum
dash lime juice, freshly squeezed
dash lemon juice, freshly squeezed
25 ml (1 oz) pineapple juice
25 ml (1 oz) orange Curaçao
25 ml (1 oz) apricot brandy
25 ml (1 oz) orgeat syrup (or hazelnut liqueur)
2 dashes of Angostura bitters
2 mint leaves
sprig of mint, to garnish
slice of pineapple, to garnish

Method

Pour the rum, lime, lemon and pineapple juice, orange Curaçao, apricot brandy, orgeat syrup and Angostura bitters into shaker with ice. Add the mint leaves and shake well. Serve with a sprig of mint and a slice of pineapple.

HARRY'S NEW YORK BAR,

Paris

This is yet another Hemingway haunt and a bar that also played host to Coco Chanel, Humphrey Bogart, Rita Hayworth and the Duke of Windsor. It lays claim to the invention of several cocktails, including the Bloody Mary, the Sidecar and French 75.

French 75

Ingredients

50 ml (2 oz) gin
25 ml (1 oz) lemon juice, freshly squeezed
25 ml (1 oz) sugar syrup
champagne

Method

Shake the gin, lemon juice and sugar syrup with ice and strain into a highball glass. Top up with champagne.

LA BODEGUITA DEL MEDIO,

Havana

The Mojito was supposedly invented in Havana in 1942. Our man Hemingway crops up again, this time with a handwritten endorsement of the Mojito, which still hangs on the wall of this iconic bar.

Mojito

Ingredients

2 teaspoons caster (superfine) sugar
50 ml (2 oz) lime juice, freshly squeezed
6 mint leaves
75 ml (2¾ oz) rum
soda water
sprig of mint, to garnish

Method

Muddle the caster sugar, lime juice and mint leaves in a highball glass. Add the rum and fill with crushed ice, top up with soda water and garnish with mint.

HARRY'S BAR,
Venice

This is the undisputed home of the Bellini. Harry's Bar was opened by Giuseppe Cipriani in 1931 and he gave the Bellini its name because the colour reminded him of a saint's toga in a painting by the 15th-century artist Giovanni Bellini.

Peach Bellini

Ingredients

1 part peach purée
3 parts champagne

Method

To make the purée simply stone some peaches and chuck them into a blender. Stir the ingredients in a mixing glass and strain into a champagne flute. Top up with more champagne if necessary.

THE CARIBE HILTON,
San Juan

Opened in 1949, The Caribe Hilton was the first Hilton hotel located outside the US. In 1954, the head barman Monchito was given the task of creating a signature drink for the hotel and the Piña Colada was born.

Piña Colada

Ingredients

50 ml (2 oz) white rum
25 ml (1 oz) dark rum
75 ml (2¾ oz) pineapple juice
50 ml (2 oz) coconut cream
pineapple wedges, to garnish

Method

Use a blender to process some crushed ice, the white rum, dark rum, pineapple juice and coconut cream until smooth. Pour into a highball glass and garnish with pineapple wedges.

FAIRMONT HOTEL,

Formerly The Grunewald

New Orleans

One of the first American cocktails, the Sazerac was created in New Orleans by Antoine Peychaud and named after his favourite French brandy, Sazerac de Forge et Fils. The Grunewald Hotel was built in 1893 and subsequently earned the exclusive rights to serve the Sazerac. In 1965 the hotel was renamed the Fairmont Hotel.

Sazerac

Ingredients

dash of absinthe
50 ml (2 oz) cognac
1 teaspoon sugar
3 dashes of Angostura bitters

Method

Splash the absinthe into a glass and pour out. Place in the freezer to chill. Stir the rest of the ingredients into a mixing glass with ice. Strain into the absinthe-coated glass.

BELLE EPOQUE, HÔTEL MÉTROPOLE,
Luxembourg

Luxembourg is the home of the Black Russian: it was created in 1949 by Gustave Tops in honour of the then US ambassador to the country. The Metropole is the only 19th-century hotel still in existence in Brussels today.

Black Russian

Ingredients

50 ml (2 oz) vodka
25 ml (1 oz) Kahlúa

Method

Pour the vodka and Kahlúa over ice into a tumbler and stir gently.

CHAPTER 8
HOW TO THROW
A COCKTAIL PARTY

A good party is one in which bad things happen.
Lewd jokes, confessions, dirty dancing, break-ups, make-ups, fleeting embraces and stolen kisses. You don't want a forgettable evening of nibbles and drinks. You want something that teeters constantly on the edge of chaos.

Everything else in this book has shown you how to be a gentleman. Now is the time to unleash your inner cad. You only have to get it right once. The kudos achieved by throwing one legendary party will ensure your popularity for many years to come.

Like a good cocktail, a good party is a carefully blended mixture of ingredients.

INSPIRATION

Let the example of London's Hellfire Club be your guide. It was a secret society for 'persons of quality' who wished to take part in immoral acts, and members were drawn from the highest echelons of society and politics. By day, the club's founder, Lord Wharton, was considered a true gentleman right down to his velvet-gloved fingertips – a respected politician and man of letters. But come the night he was an infamous drunkard, rioter, infidel and rake.

Hellfire Punch

Ingredients

50 ml (2 oz) Sailor Jerry rum
50 ml (2 oz) ginger beer
2 dashes Tabasco
Pilsner beer
wedge of fresh lime, to garnish

Method

Pour the rum, ginger beer and Tabasco into a highball glass over ice. Top up with Pilsner and garnish with lime.

Stinger

Ingredients

50 ml (2 oz) brandy
25 ml (1 oz) white crème de menthe

Method

Shake the brandy and crème de menthe well
over ice and strain into a martini glass.

Knickerbocker

Ingredients

50 ml (2 oz) gin
large dash dry vermouth
small dash sweet vermouth

Method

Shake the ingredients over ice and strain into
a frosted martini glass.

GIRLS

Inform some attractive girls, from a variety of different social groups, that you will be having a party and ask them to bring their friends. Tell them there will be a fantastic array of cocktails specially made. Name a few in their honour. And tell them that there will be attractive men there. Tell your male friends to bring their own booze.

Fish House Punch

Ingredients

(serves 20)
note: needs to be prepared the night before
400 ml (14 oz) sugar syrup
400 ml (14 oz) cold water
300 ml (10½ oz) lemon juice, freshly squeezed
500 ml (18 oz) rum
1 bottle (700 ml/25 oz) cognac
100 ml (3½ oz) peach brandy
lemon slices, to garnish

Method

Stir the sugar syrup and water together in a large bowl. Add the lemon juice, rum, cognac and peach brandy. Put in the fridge and chill overnight. Freeze a 2 litre (4 pint) block of ice overnight. Place in the punch bowl and pour the punch over it. Garnish with lemon slices.

Recipe courtesy of Bompas and Parr

Paloma

Ingredients

75 ml (2¼ oz) fresh grapefruit juice
50 ml (2 oz) silver grade or blanco tequila
15 ml (½ oz) lime juice, freshly squeezed
15 ml (½ oz) agave nectar
sea salt
soda water
slice of lime, to garnish

Method

Shake grapefruit juice, tequila, lime juice
and agave nectar well over ice. Strain into
an ice-filled Collins glass rimmed with sea
salt. Top up with soda water and add a slice
of lime to garnish.

Laura Jane

Ingredients

25 ml (1 oz) pear eau de vie brandy
15 ml (½ oz) lemon juice, freshly squeezed
25 ml (1 oz) Tuaca
75 ml (2¾ oz) champagne

Method

Shake the eau de vie, lemon juice and Tuaca
well over ice. Strain into a champagne glass
and top up with champagne.

SOCIAL FRICTION

Opposites not only attract, they also create positive energy: especially when they've got a few drinks inside them. Try to get a blend of young and old, and people from a variety of ethnicities, countries, industries and cultures. Get the fashion PR into a conversation with the atomic scientist, the public school fop with the Essex hairdresser, and see what happens.

Arsenal Punch

Ingredients

(serves 20)
950 ml (33 oz) strong black tea
560 ml (20 oz) orange juice
290 ml (10 oz) lemon juice, freshly squeezed
50 ml (2 oz) Bénédictine
750 ml (26 oz) red wine
950 ml (33 oz) rye whisky
290 ml (10 oz) brandy
560 ml (20 oz) Jamaican dark rum
lemon slices, to garnish

Method

Stir the tea, orange and lemon juice, and Bénédictine together in a large bowl. Add the wine, whisky and brandy. Put in the fridge and chill for 2 hours. Freeze a 2 litre (4 pint) block of ice overnight. Place in the punch bowl and pour the punch over it. Garnish with the lemon slices.

Tom and Jerry

Ingredients

1 egg, separated
25 ml (1 oz) dark rum
25 ml (1 oz) brandy
1 teaspoon sugar
boiling water
ground nutmeg, to garnish

Method

Beat the egg white and yolk separately, then mix together in a heat-resistant wine glass. Add the remaining ingredients to the egg mixture and top up with boiling water. Sprinkle with nutmeg.

Brandy Flip

Ingredients

50 ml (2 oz) brandy
1 egg
dash of sugar syrup

Method

Stir the ingredients over ice and strain into a wine glass.

GO SOMEWHERE ELSE FIRST

Gather a group of friends and go to your favourite cocktail bar first. This means you are not sitting around at home waiting for the party to start as people arrive in dribs and drabs. Instead, you are bringing the party back home with you and making it start with a bang.

Champagne punch

Ingredients

(serves 20)

1.5 litres (53 oz) chilled champagne

1.5 litres (53 oz) chilled lemonade

400 ml (14 oz) chilled vodka

400 ml (14 oz) Malibu

5 limes, thinly sliced

500 g (18 oz) frozen raspberries

625 ml (22 oz) fresh passion fruit pulp

Method

Combine the ingredients in a large bowl. Pour into jugs, add ice and serve.

Kingsley Amis' Milk Punch

Ingredients

frozen milk cubes
25 ml (1 oz) brandy
25 ml (1 oz) bourbon
100 ml (3½ oz) milk
25 ml (1 oz) sugar syrup

Method

Put the milk into an ice tray and freeze.
Mix the brandy, bourbon, milk and sugar syrup
and drop a few frozen milk cubes into a jug.
Good for the morning after!

Recipe courtesy of Bompass and Parr

Americano

Ingredients

25 ml (1 oz) Campari
25 ml (1 oz) sweet vermouth
soda water
slice of orange, to garnish

Method

Pour the spirits into a highball glass and
top up with soda water. Garnish with a
slice of orange.

INTRODUCE THE ROGUE ELEMENT

Just as a good Bloody Mary needs a bit of kick and spice to it, so too does your party. When you are at the cocktail bar get one of your female companions to befriend a group of attractive girls (strangers) and invite them to your party. Offer to pay for their taxi and get in it with them.

True Friendship Punch

Ingredients

(serves 20)
450 ml (16 oz) brandy
450 ml (16 oz) dark rum
450 ml (16 oz) whisky
125 ml (4 oz) orange Curaçao
75 ml (2¾ oz) lime juice, freshly squeezed
135 g (5 oz) caster (superfine) sugar
1 teaspoon Angostura bitters
700ml (25 oz) soda water
1 orange, sliced
1 lemon, sliced
peeled cucumber skin, to garnish
herbs and spices of your choice, to garnish
(such as cinnamon, nutmeg, ginger etc)

Method

Put the brandy, rum, whisky, Curaçao, lime juice, sugar and bitters into a large bowl. Put in the fridge for 2 hours. Just before serving pour the chilled ingredients over a large block of ice, add the soda water and spinkle with the herbs and spices.

Recipe courtesy of Bompas and Parr

Rum Cove

Ingredients

50 ml (2 oz) white rum
1 teaspoon grenadine
15 ml (½ oz) lime juice, freshly squeezed

Method

Shake the ingredients over ice and strain into a martini glass.

Planter's Punch

Ingredients

50 ml (2 oz) dark rum
25 ml (1 oz) lime juice, freshly squeezed
sugar syrup
2 dashes of Angostura bitters
soda water
lime wedge, to garnish

Method

Shake the rum and lime juice over ice, and add a dash of sugar syrup and Angostura bitters. Shake and strain into a highball glass filled with ice. Top up with soda and garnish with a lime wedge.

DJ

Get a DJ in. Don't just fiddle around on a computer. A good DJ actually doing some mixing adds to the sense of occasion. Make them play party music – Rolling Stones, Jay-Z, Michael Jackson, Rick James – nothing too cool or niche. Remember, you want French grandad to get jiggy with the Japanese divorcee, and he's hardly going to do that to bloodcurdling drum and bass, is he? But he might just do it to Super Freak.

Grantini

Ingredients

(serves 4)
300 ml (10½ oz) prosecco
150 ml (5 oz) Stolichnaya Gold
traditional pink lemonade
1 pear, quartered lengthways

Method

Chill the prosecco and vodka in a freezer for 1–2 hours. Half fill a large jug with big chunks of ice. Pour in the prosecco and vodka, and top up with pink lemonade. Add the pear.

Gin Rickey

Ingredients

50 ml (2 oz) gin
15 ml (½ oz) lime juice, freshly squeezed
15 ml (½ oz) sugar syrup
soda water
lime wedge, to garnish

Method

Pour the gin, lime juice and sugar syrup into a highball glass filled with ice. Top up with soda water and garnish with a lime wedge.

Brandy Alexander

Ingredients

50 ml (2 oz) brandy
25 ml (1 oz) white crème de cacao
25 ml (1 oz) dark crème de cacao
15ml (½ oz) fresh single cream
ground nutmeg, to garnish

Method

Shake the ingredients well over ice and strain into a frosted martini glass. Garnish with a sprinkle of nutmeg.

VALUABLES

Inviting total strangers into your home is not without its perils. How is the drunkard fiddling around on your funny-looking tape machine at 4 a.m. to know that it is in fact a vintage Bang & Olufsen reel-to-reel player? And how do you inform the couple getting hot and heavy against your Robin Day sideboard that her wedding ring is making a huge scratch on the precious oak veneer?

Prohibition Punch

Ingredients

125 ml (4 oz) Pimm's No. 1
50 ml (2 oz) Hendrick's gin
300 ml (10½ oz) ginger ale
300 ml (10 oz) ginger beer
4–5 dashes of Angostura bitters
squeeze of lime
sliced cucumber, to garnish
strawberries, to garnish
chopped pears, to garnish

Method

Combine all the ingredients in a punch bowl and stir until frothy. Garnish with sliced cucumbers, strawberries and pears. Top up with ice cubes and serve.

Pisco Sour

Ingredients

75 ml (2¾ oz) Pisco
25 ml (1 oz) lime juice, freshly squeezed
1 tablespoon sugar
1 egg white
dash of Angostura bitters

Method

Put the Pisco, lime juice, sugar and egg white
into a blender and process for 30 seconds
or until frothy. Add some ice and process
for one minute. Pour into a highball glass
and add the bitters to the foam before serving.

Imperial

Ingredients

25 ml (1 oz) gin
25 ml (1 oz) dry vermouth
dash of Angostura bitters
dash of maraschino juice
1 green olive, to garnish

Method

Stir all the ingredients over ice and strain
into a martini glass. Garnish with the olive.

YOUR TEAM

As a host you want to be busy having a good time and introducing people to one another. Assign several trusted male friends with some of the other tasks. Your friend might moan about being put on Mojito-mixing duty, but tell him that girls love Mojitos and that he will get to meet every single attractive woman in the course of the night. Lucky boy.

Xalapa Punch

Ingredients

(serves 20)
1 litre (2 pints) strong black tea
grated orange peel
500 ml (18 oz) sugar syrup (or to taste)
375 ml (13 oz) rum
375 ml (13 oz) calvados
375 ml (13 oz) dry red wine
orange slices, to garnish
lemon slices, to garnish

Method

Add hot water to the tea and allow to brew for at least five minutes. Mix hot tea and grated orange peel together in a saucepan and allow to cool. Add the sugar and mix until dissolved. Pour the other ingredients into the mix with a block of ice and chill for several hours. Garnish with orange and lemon slices.

Pink Gin

Ingredients

dash of Angostura bitters
50 ml (2 oz) gin

Method

Coat the inside of a martini glass with
Angostura bitters. Add the gin and some
ice and serve.

Whisky Mac

Ingredients

50 ml (2 oz) scotch
50 ml (2 oz) Stone's Green Ginger Wine

Method

Pour the whisky and ginger wine over ice into
a tumbler. Stir and serve.

FOOD

Nobody has ever remembered a party for the quality of the food. They remember who had sex with whom and who confessed something they shouldn't have. So don't get too carried away as nobody will care. At the very least provide posh crisps. At the most get your local restaurant to prepare some snacks.

Brandy Punch

Ingredients

(serves 20)
225 ml (8 oz) sugar syrup
225 ml (8 oz) Curaçao
450 ml (16 oz) lemon juice, freshly squeezed
450 ml (16 oz) orange juice, freshly squeezed
50 ml (2 oz) grenadine
2 bottles of cognac (750 ml/26 oz each)
700 ml (25 oz) soda water

Method
Mix and chill the ingredients in the fridge for 1–2 hours, then pour over a 2 litre (4 pint) block of ice. Add the soda water to serve.

Gin & Ting

Ingredients

50 ml (2 oz) gin
50 ml (2 oz) sweet red vermouth

Method

Stir the gin and vermouth well over ice and strain into a frosted martini glass.

Bourbon Highball

Ingredients

50 ml (2 oz) bourbon
ginger ale
twist of lemon peel, to garnish

Method

Pour the bourbon into a highball glass filled with ice and top up with ginger beer. Garnish with a twist of lemon.

COCKTAIL PARTY CHECKLIST

1. Slice lemons and limes beforehand. Drunkards with blades ruin parties.
2. Parsimony is absolutely unforgivable. Buy as much alcohol as possible.
3. Get as much ice as possible and then double it.
4. Get an interesting-looking receptacle. A traditional baby pram filled with ice makes for a good champagne cooler.
5. Pre-chill as many glasses as possible. Get extra ones in.
6. Provide a dress code. Don't be too specific but try to make sure everyone has made some kind of effort, the men especially.
7. Scented candles will make even the drabbest flat look like a place where seduction can take place.
8. Don't forget to prepare the outside spaces. Get heaters, garden furniture and lanterns.
9. Don't try to make everyone a cocktail – too fiddly. Instead, provide ingredients and equipment for people to make their own. Also prepare punches.
10. If all else fails, hire your favourite barman to do everything.

Hot Toddy

Ingredients

50 ml (2 oz) whisky
1 tablespoon honey
boiling water
5 cloves
1 lemon slice
1 cinnamon stick
15 ml (½ oz) lemon juice, freshly squeezed

Method

Pour the whisky and honey into a heatproof tumbler. Half fill with boiling water and stir until blended. Spear the five cloves into the skin of the lemon slice and place in the glass. Add the cinnamon stick and lemon juice and stir again.

CHAPTER 9
SEDUCTION

A good cocktail bar is the ideal venue to conduct a romance. Look out for speakeasies located in an unloved part of town and housed behind a deliberately scruffy, anonymous-looking door. The excellent Nightjar on City Road in London is one such venue.

While your date may initially be disappointed or even a little scared, once you have escorted her past the rubbish kebab shops, tramps and down a flight of stairs – voilà! – a 1930s speakeasy bar awaits you both. The contrast between the mean streets outside and the seductive glamour inside means that a chap is 1—0 up before he has even taken off his coat.

Wherever you go and whoever your date is, successful seduction requires attention to detail.

CHOOSE THE VENUE

You want somewhere that feels suitably clandestine. Low lighting, tasteful and distinctive décor, attentive staff and a similarly attractive clientele should serve to create an atmosphere far removed from your local pub or bar chain.

Leroi

Ingredients

35 ml (1⅓ oz) Knob Creek Bourbon
25 ml (1 oz) sloe gin
1 egg yolk
15 ml (½ oz) grenadine
1 teaspoon crème fraiche
a squeeze of lemon juice (or to taste)

Method

Shake the ingredients with ice, strain and serve in a coupe glass.

Recipe courtesy of Nightjar

BRIBE THE STAFF

There's a scene in *Goodfellas* in which Ray Liotta guides Lorraine Bracco through the basement of the Copacabana club directly to the best seat in the house, where they are greeted with a bottle of cold champagne. This is the ultimate entrance, but how did he do it? With charm and dollar bills. Staff will be willing accomplices in your seduction and the offer of a generous tip guarantees cooperation. Strike up a rapport with the person who will be looking after you that evening.

Julep

Ingredients

40 ml (1½ oz) Four Roses Small Batch Bourbon
20 ml (¾ oz) apricot-infused brandy
3 mint leaves, bruised

Method

Add the bourbon, brandy, crushed ice and mint to a small shaker or julep tin. Muddle hard with the end of a bar spoon to extract the mint oils. Serve in the shaker or tin.

Recipe courtesy of Nightjar

BOOK A TABLE

Always reserve the best seat in the house. Ideally, you should sit next to or adjacent to one another, in a relatively quiet area: this is more intimate but not so removed that it is impossible to get the attention of the table service. The worst tables are near thoroughfares and walkways because of the likelihood of spilled drinks and interrupted conversations.

Valencia

Ingredients

20 ml (¾ oz) blood orange juice
20 ml (¾ oz) mandarin juice
15 ml (½ oz) apricot-infused brandy
dash of orange bitters
champagne

Method

Shake the ingredients together and serve straight up in a champagne flute. Top up with champagne.

EN ROUTE

If you have been dining with your date beforehand, phone before you leave the restaurant and say that you would like your table to be ready in 10 minutes. Find out what her favourite cocktail is and ask them to start mixing hers and yours upon your arrival. This means you bypass the queue and have your drinks waiting for you when you sit down. This is an entrance of which any Goodfella would be proud.

Airmail

Ingredients

15 ml (½ oz) brown rum
15 ml (½ oz) orange blossom honey water
muddled mint leaves
½ juice of lime, freshly squeezed
champagne

Method

Shake the ingredients together and serve in a champagne flute. Top up with champagne.

Recipe courtesy of Nightjar

UPON ARRIVAL

GIVE HER THE BEST SEAT

Always lead your date to the table so she realises that you are taking her to the best seat. Make sure she gets the most comfortable seat with the best view of the band or piano player.

Dan the Man

Ingredients

dash of dry vermouth
50 ml (2 oz) gin
1 cocktail onion, to garnish

Method

Fill a mixing glass with ice and add a dash of dry vermouth. Stir until the vermouth has coated the ice, then strain out the liquid. Top up a mixing glass with ice, add gin and stir until the glass is frosted. Pour into a tumbler and garnish with a cocktail onion on a toothpick.

ORDERING WITH CLASS

Like a restaurant they will have house specials and new inventions. Ask the waitress to talk through them. Better still, familiarise yourself with the menu beforehand and guide your date through it. Looking like you know what you're doing is not only impressive but it will also make her feel more comfortable.

Chocolate Martini

Ingredients

cocoa, to garnish
3 milk chocolate buttons (drops)
30 ml (2 oz) white crème de cacao
30 ml (2 oz) vodka

Method

Dust the rim of a martini glass and place the chocolate buttons in the bottom. Shake the crème de cacao and vodka with ice, and strain into the glass.

BE GENEROUS

BUT DON'T BE A CAD (YET)

Place your glass far away enough so that you can't knock it over. Be generous and offer your date a taste of your drink before you try it. As you take your first sip, raise your glass in her direction, arch one eyebrow, look her in the eye and smile devilishly.

Offer her water and be aware of how much she's had to drink. If she gets too drunk then it will be your fault and she will blame you. Under no circumstances get drunker than her.

Godfather

Ingredients

50 ml (1 oz) scotch
25 ml (½ oz) amaretto

Method

Pour the ingredients into a tumbler over ice and stir.

Between the Sheets

Ingredients

25 ml (1 oz) Hennessy Fine de Cognac
25 ml (1 oz) Diplomático Reserva Rum
25 ml (1 oz) Cointreau
25 ml (1 oz) lemon juice
1 teaspoon caster (superfine) sugar
   (or simple syrup)
lemon wedge, to garnish

Method

Shake the ingredients with ice, strain and serve in a coupe glass. Garnish with a lemon wedge on the rim.

Recipe courtesy of Nightjar

HOME TIME

SECOND DATE

You've shared a kiss, are a bit tipsy
and having lots of fun – this is a good time
to arrange a second date.

THE BILL

If it's getting late in the evening, what
time do they close? You don't want the bill
foisted upon you. It looks much better to
ask in advance. Better still, settle the bill
when you go to the bathroom and pay it
before you sit back down. To talk about
money during a date is terribly vulgar. For
God's sake don't go Dutch.

The Wibble

Ingredients

50 ml (2 oz) Plymouth Navy sloe gin
25 ml (1 oz) pink grapefruit juice
1 teaspoon lemon juice, freshly squeezed
1 teaspoon sugar syrup
1 teaspoon Muroise

Method

Shake the ingredients with ice and strain. Serve
in a coupe glass.

Recipe courtesy of Nightjar

JUST ASK

If you find yourself without a companion, ask politely and in some bars staff will introduce you to eligible ladies. And if you are with friends, they might seat your party next to a table with an equal number of ladies, although it's best to go with just one wingman.

Tom Collins

Ingredients

75 ml (2¾ oz) gin
50 ml (2 oz) lemon juice, freshly squeezed
15 ml (½ oz) sugar syrup
splash of soda water
lemon slice, to garnish

Method

Shake the gin, lemon juice and sugar syrup over ice. Strain into a tumbler, add the soda water and garnish with a lemon slice.

JUST DON'T

Never send drinks over. You may as well make a paper plane out of a £50 note with your phone number written on it. Avoid any unnecessary public humiliation for both of you, as it will hinder your chances with other eligible ladies who might have liked the look of you.

Rusty Nail

Ingredients

25 ml (1 oz) scotch
25 ml (1 oz) Drambuie (or to taste)

Method

Combine the ingredients in a tumbler over ice and stir.

CHAPTER 10
BUSINESS AS USUAL

Careers and fortunes have been built on the back
of a man's ability to show people a good time.
Hedge funds often employ a person whose primary
job is to entertain clients. And while advertising is
no longer as booze-drenched as it used to be, much
of an ad man's time will be spent getting to know
the clients they work for.

Whatever you do, wherever you are in the world,
one day your charm, sophistication and good taste
will be put to the test in a professional context.
This is how to win.

TREAT IT LIKE IT'S A DATE

Are they a man or a woman? How old are they? What kind of place are they going to like? And how are you going to get there? It is in many ways like seduction. Prepare the ground and pay attention to the details as you would on a date (see pages 112–121).

Respect on a Business Level

Ingredients

50 ml (2 oz) reposado tequila
25 ml (1 oz) Aperol
3 dashes of celery bitters
twist of orange peel, to garnish

Method

Vigorously stir the tequila, Aperol and bitters over ice for 30 seconds. Strain into an ice-filled tumbler. Twist the orange peel over the drink to release the oils and rub it over the rim of the glass before using it as garnish.

Bro Juice

Ingredients

10 ml (⅓ oz) lemon juice, freshly squeezed
35 ml (1⅓ oz) bourbon
25 ml (1 oz) apricot liqueur
25 ml (1 oz) apple juice
twist of orange peel, to garnish

Method

Shake the ingredients over ice and strain into a martini glass. Garnish with an orange twist.

Amber Mist

Ingredients

3 cloves
25 ml (1 oz) sugar syrup
75 ml (2¾ oz) vodka
25 ml (1 oz) Grand Marnier
50 ml (2 oz) strong Earl Grey tea
piec of orange peel, to garnish

Method

Muddle the cloves and sugar syrup in a shaker and pour in the vodka, Grand Marnier and cold Earl Grey. Shake and strain into a coupe glass, then squeeze the orange zest over the top to release the orange oils.

MATCH THE VALUES

Match the venue to the values of the organisation. If you are trying to win business from Dunhill then somewhere like the Savoy is entirely correct.
Less so if your client is a budget airline. The same goes for ordering drinks. Huge magnums of champagne will not impress people who work for Greenpeace, whereas it might be just the thing for a group of investment bankers.

Alabama Slammer

Ingredients

25 ml (1 oz) Southern Comfort
15 ml (½ oz) amaretto
15 ml (½ oz) sloe gin
splash of orange juice
wedge of orange, to garnish

Method

Pour the ingredients into a highball glass filled with ice and stir. Garnish with a wedge of orange.

SOCIALISING

The point of entertaining clients is primarily social. You're trying to build rapport and get to know them better in order to create a better working relationship. Business is very rarely concluded over cocktails, but a relaxed and stylish cocktail bar could be just the place to observe the dynamic within an organisation.

Kir Royale

Ingredients

a few dashes of crème de cassis
glass of champagne

Method

Coat the inside of a chilled champagne flute with the crème de cassis, then fill with champagne.

ADD SOME INTRIGUE

People always like to be delighted and intrigued by new experiences but nobody wants to feel like grandad at a disco. If your client is used to going to the Wolseley in London or the Four Seasons in New York, surprising them with the latest pop-up bar or speakeasy may be an exciting change from the norm. It's up to you to strike the balance.

Rosita

Ingredients

50 ml (2 oz) reposada tequila
50 ml (2 oz) Campari
25 ml (1 oz) sweet vermouth
25 ml (1 oz) dry vermouth
1 dash of Angostura bitters
twist of lemon or lime peel, to garnish

Method

Stir the ingredients in a shaker with ice cubes, strain into a glass filled with ice and garnish with lemon or lime peel.

Watermelon Man

Ingredients

½ juice of lime, freshly squeezed
15 g (½ oz) watermelon
25 ml (1 oz) gin
tonic water

Method

Squeeze the lime into a tumbler and drop
it into the glass. Chop the watermelon and
add to the glass with some ice cubes. Pour
the gin over the mix and top up with chilled
tonic water.

Blood Money

Ingredients

2 clementines, juiced
1 teaspoon Campari
prosecco

Method

Pour the clementine juice and Campari
into a tumbler. Top up with prosecco.

SAY LESS THAN IS NECESSARY

Say as little as possible. Instead, listen. Psychologists have conducted tests to discover which people are considered to be the most charming and interesting. It is always the person who speaks least. Listening means that you are able to glean that vital piece of information which could tip the balance in your favour.

Margarita

Ingredients

25 ml (1 oz) lime juice
salt, to garnish
50 ml (2 oz) white tequila
25 ml (1 oz) Cointreau

Method

Rub the rim of a champagne coupe glass with lime juice and salt. Shake the ingredients over ice and strain into the glass.

HOW TO SPOT GOOD SERVICE

A good barman or cocktail waitress is rather like the famous fictional butler Jeeves. They should magically appear when needed, but be entirely inconspicuous when not. They should be knowledgeable and remain unflustered and calm at all times. They should move with fluidity and economy, putting you and your guests at ease. They should remember who you are and be aware of the importance of the occasion.

Rhett Butler

Ingredients

50 ml (2 oz) Southern Comfort
25 ml (1 oz) orange Curaçao
25 ml (1 oz) lime juice, freshly squeezed
25 ml (1 oz) lemon juice, freshly squeezed
a twist of lemon peel, to garnish

Method

Pour the ingredients into a cocktail shaker filled with ice and shake hard. Strain into a chilled cocktail glass and garnish with a twist of lemon.

FOOD

A 12-course Michelin tasting menu might sound impressive but combine that with a few Martinis and you will soon be too tired to be a good host. If the plan is to go bar-hopping and then a nightclub think of food as merely fuel. Eat a small snack every now and then to give you the energy to keep going.

Tequila Sunrise

Ingredients

25 ml (1 oz) tequila
240 ml (8 oz) orange juice
1 teaspoon grenadine
orange wedge, to garnish

Method

Half fill a highball glass with ice cubes and add tequila. Top up with orange juice and add a teaspoon of grenadine. Garnish with a wedge of orange.

Trill Juice

Ingredients

200 ml (7 oz) vodka
200 ml (7 oz) Cointreau
600 ml (21 oz) cranberry juice
400 ml (14 oz) orange juice
peel from 2 – 3 limes
crushed ice

Method

Pour the vodka and Cointreau into a jug,
then add the cranberry juice and orange
juice. Stir well. Pour into ice-filled glasses
and garnish with the lime peel.

Bloody Bull

Ingredients

50 ml (2 oz) vodka
75 ml (2¾ oz) tomato juice
15 ml (½ oz) lemon juice
50 ml (2 oz) beef bouillon
3 dashes of Tabasco
ground black pepper and salt

Method

Shake the ingredients and strain into a
highball glass filled with crushed ice.

DRINK LIKE THEM

Different countries have different drinking cultures. In South-east Asia, someone who can drink a lot and participate in drinking games is generally considered quite impressive. Americans on the other hand drink very little.

Shirley Temple

Ingredients

25 ml (1 oz) lemon juice, freshly squeezed
25 ml (1 oz) grenadine
25 ml (1 oz) sugar syrup
150 ml (5 oz) ginger ale
orange slice, to garnish

Method

Shake the lemon juice, grenadine and sugar syrup vigorously over cracked ice and strain into a highball glass half-filled with ice. Top up with ginger ale and garnish with an orange slice.

PLAN AHEAD

Decide upfront whether you want to get drunk or not. Don't leave it to the moment. The best plans are the ones you make sober, not when you are three sheets to the wind.

Red Apple Sunset

Ingredients

50 ml (2 oz) apple juice
50 ml (2 oz) grapefruit juice
dash of grenadine

Method

Shake the apple juice, grapefruit juice and grenadine well over ice. Strain into a chilled cocktail glass.

THE MORNING AFTER

If, despite your best intentions, you do overindulge in cocktails, never fear! This hair of the dog will sort you out in no time.

Hair of the Dog

Ingredients

50 ml (2 oz) scotch
50 ml (2 oz) single (pouring) cream
3 teaspoons honey

Method

Shake the ingredients well over ice and strain into a martini glass.

Virgin Mary

Ingredients

75 ml (2¾ oz) tomato juice
15 ml (½ oz) lemon juice
3 dashes of Worcestershire sauce
3 dashes of Tabasco
celery salt
ground white pepper

Method

Shake the ingredients over ice and strain into a highball glass filled with ice cubes.

Prairie Oyster

Ingredients

1 whole egg
50 ml (2 oz) vodka
2 dashes of vinegar
1 teaspoon Worcestershire sauce
1 tablespoon tomato juice
2 dashes of Tabasco
salt and pepper

Method

Crack the egg into a highball glass, making sure you don't break the yolk. Add the remaining ingredients. Drink in one gulp.

ALFRED TONG

was born in London in 1978 and has lived in South London, Essex, Los Angeles and Hong Kong. He studied Journalism at the London College of Fashion and has written for *The Times*, *Esquire* and *Time Out London*. This is his first book.

JACK HUGHES

was born in 1989 and lives South London. He attended Kingston University where he studied Illustration & Animation, quickly signing up with illustration agency YCN upon graduation in 2011. Recent clients include *Google*, *Sunday Telegraph*, *Computer Arts* and *Time Out London*.

INDEX